W9-BQZ-220

00 30 0323061 6

HAYNER PUBLIC LIBRARY DISTRICT
ALTON, ILLINOIS

OVERDUES 10 PER DAY. MAXIMUM FINE
COST OF BOOKS. LOST OR DAMAGED BOOKS
ADDITIONAL $1.00 SERVICE CHARGE.

BRANCH

Science Alive!
the
Human Body

CRABTREE
Publishing Company
www.crabtreebooks.com

HAYNER PUBLIC LIBRARY DISTRICT
ALTON, ILLINOIS

How to use this book

Each chapter begins with experiments, followed by the explanation of the scientific concepts used in the experiments. Each experiment is graded according to its difficulty level. A level 4 or 5 means adult assistance is advised. Difficult words are in boldface and explained in the glossary on page 32.

Crabtree Publishing
www.crabtreebooks.com

PMB 16A, 350 Fifth Avenue,
Suite 3308, New York
New York 10118

612 Welland Avenue,
St. Catharines, Ontario
Canada L2M 5V6

**Published in 2003
by Crabtree Publishing Company**

Published with Times Editions
Copyright © 2003 by Times Media Private Limited

All North American rights reserved. No part of this book may be reproduced, stored in a retrieval system, or transmitted in any form or by any means—electronic, mechanical, photocopying, recording, or otherwise—without the prior written permission of Crabtree Publishing Company, except for the inclusion of brief quotations in an acknowledged review.

Series originated and designed by
TIMES EDITIONS
An imprint of Times Media Private Limited
A member of the Times Publishing Group

Coordinating Editor: Ellen Rodger
Project Editor: Carrie Gleason
Production Coordinator: Rosie Gowsell
Series Writers: Darlene Lauw, Lim Cheng Puay
Series Editor: Oh Hwee Yen
Title Editor: Oh Hwee Yen
Series Designer: Rosie Francis
Series Picture Researcher: Susan Jane Manuel

Cataloging-in-Publication Data
Lauw, Darlene.
    The human body / Darlene Lauw and Lim Cheng Puay.
        p. cm. — (Science alive!)
    Includes index.
    Summary: Introduces concepts related to human anatomy and physiology through various activities and projects.
    ISBN 0-7787-0568-4 — ISBN 0-7787-0614-1
    1. Human physiology—Juvenile literature. 2. Body, Human—Juvenile literature. [1. Human physiology. 2. Human anatomy. 3. Body, Human.]
    I. Lim, Cheng Puay. II. Title. III. Series.
    QP37 .L28 2003
    612—dc21
                                                                2002013741
                                                                            LC

Picture Credits
Marc Crabtree: cover; Art Directors & Trip Photo Library: 6, 7 (middle), 10 (bottom), 14 (top), 19 (bottom), 26–27 (bottom), 30; Bes Stock: 1, 11, 14–15 (bottom), 18, 22, 23, 27 (middle), 31 (top); Getty Images/Hulton Archive: 15 (top); MC Picture Library: 7 (top), 10 (top), 19 (middle), 27; Photobank Photolibrary/Singapore: 31 (bottom); Science Photo Library: 19 (top), 23 (top)

Printed and bound in Malaysia
1 2 3 4 5 6—0S—07 06 05 04 03 02

j612
LAU

AEI -0/22

INTRODUCTION

The human body works in many amazing ways. Our lungs and heart work like engines, pumping blood and oxygen to different parts of the body. We find out about the world around us through our five senses: taste, touch, hearing, sight, and smell. How do we walk without falling? What happens to food after we eat it? Find out the answers to these questions and more by reading and doing the fun experiments in this book!

Contents

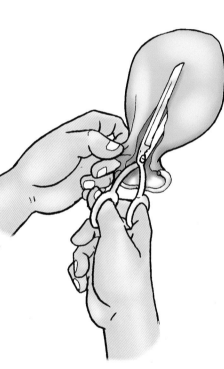

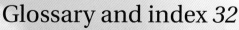

Our eyes and ears

Can you imagine a day without seeing or hearing? We would not be able to find our way around or hear what our friends tell us. Sound reaches our ears through vibrating **molecules** of air. What happens to the sounds after they reach our ears?

Drum in the ear

Difficult – 5
– 4
Moderate – 3
– 2
Easy – 1

You will need:
- Scissors
- A plastic bag
- A glass jar
- Elastic bands
- A handful of uncooked rice
- A metal baking tray
- A metal ruler

1 Using the scissors, cut out a piece from the plastic bag. Make sure the piece is wide enough to cover the mouth of the jar.

2 Stretch the plastic piece tightly over the mouth of the jar, and secure it in place with the elastic bands.

3 Place the rice on top of the piece of plastic.

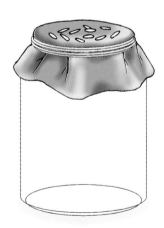

4 Hold the baking tray next to the jar, then bang on it with the ruler. What happens to the rice when you make that loud noise?

4

Our eyes capture images and send signals to the brain. Did you know that there is one tiny blind spot in your eyes? See for yourself in this activity!

Difficult — 5
— 4
Moderate — 3
— 2
Easy — 1

You will need:
- Pencil crayons
- A sheet of paper

Blind spot

1 Draw an apple on the left side and an orange on the right side of the paper, each about ¹/₂ inch (1 cm) wide and 3.5 inches (9 cm) apart.

2 Hold the paper at arms' length. Close your left eye and stare at the apple with your right eye. You should still be able to see the orange.

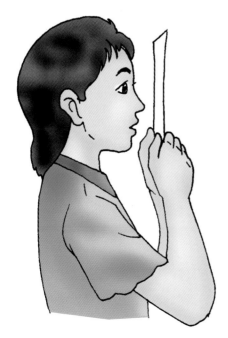

3 Now, keeping your eye on the apple, slowly bring the paper closer to your face. At a certain distance, the orange disappears!

5

Hearing things

When you struck the tray with the ruler in the *Drum in the Ear* experiment, you created sound waves. Sound waves are created when molecules of air surrounding an object vibrate, and are pushed farther apart in the form of waves. The rice in the experiment jumped because each grain received energy, or the ability to do work, from the moving air molecules. Inside our ears are eardrums, which are thin pieces of skin that act like the plastic in the experiment. When sound waves reach our eardrums, the vibrating air molecules force our eardrums to move.

Behind the eardrum are the ossicles, which are made up of three tiny bones. Sounds, or vibrations, that the eardrum receives travel through these bones to the cochlea, which is deep in the ear. The cochlea is a small, curled tube filled with liquid. Thousands of tiny hairs line the inner surface of the cochlea. These hairs are called cilia hairs. When sound vibrations reach the liquid in the cochlea, the liquid starts to vibrate, making the cilia hairs move. The hairs then change the vibrations into **nerve signals** that the brain identifies as a noise.

Sounds can be blocked by objects. This is why you can hear your friend when she cups her hands around your ear and whispers into it. Her hands block off sound around you, and allows your ear to hear what your friend is saying.

Seeing things

The colored part of our eyes, the iris, has **muscles** that control the amount of light entering the pupil. The pupil is the dark spot in the iris that allows light into the retina. The light goes into the lens, which focuses the image of what we see onto the retina, a small area with light-sensitive **cells**. The cells change the light to nerve signals that are sent to the brain. The brain then interprets the signals as images.

There are no light-sensitive cells at the back of the eye where nerves and blood pass through the retina. This area is known as the blind spot. In the *Blind Spot* experiment, the orange disappeared as you drew the paper closer to your face because the image fell on the blind spot on the retina!

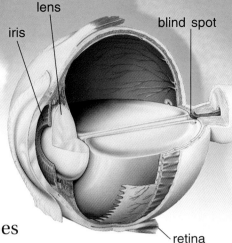

iris — lens — blind spot — retina

QUIZTIME

Which is the smallest bone in the human body?

Answer: The stirrup, a bone that is part of the ossicles. The stirrup is about 0.13 inches (0.3 cm) long and weighs only 0.15 ounces (4.7 g).

Did you know?

The spinal cord is a system of nerves that runs from the brain all the way down the back. Nerves branch out from the spinal cord to the rest of the body. This is called the nervous system. Nerves are made up of **nerve cells** that have branch-like tentacles that connect to other nerve cells and muscles. Nerve cells that carry signals from the senses to the brain are called sensory nerves. When sensory nerves detect something, a message is relayed along the nerve cells to the spinal cord, then up to the brain, where the message is identified.

DAY AND NIGHT VISION

How do nocturnal, or nighttime, animals, such as owls, leopards (*above*), and lizards, see in the dark? When we see an image, we are actually seeing light reflect, or bounce off, an object into our eyes. Many nocturnal animals have big eyes. Their pupils are also larger, which helps the eyes collect more light. The eyes of nighttime animals are packed with light-sensitive cells called rods. The eyes of daytime animals contain more color-sensitive cells called cones. Nocturnal animals see well at night, but cannot see colors well, and daytime animals see colors clearly, but have poor night vision.

Taste and smell

When we use our noses to sniff something, chemicals that make up odor molecules enter our noses and are detected by cells that send messages to our brains to tell us what we are sniffing. Can we identify food just by smell or taste?

What am I really eating?

1 Ask an adult to slice the onion, potato, apple, and pear with the vegetable knife.

■ Ask an adult for help	
Difficult	5
	4
Moderate	3
	2
Easy	1

You will need:
- An onion
- A potato
- An apple
- A pear
- A vegetable knife
- A scarf
- A friend
- A pencil or pen
- A notebook
- A cup of water

2 Tie the scarf over your friend's eyes. Hold a piece of potato under his or her nose. At the same time give him or her a piece of onion to eat.

3 Ask your friend to identify what he or she is eating and record the answer in the notebook.

4 Ask your friend to rinse his or her mouth with water before the next test. Now give your friend a bit of potato to eat while holding a piece of onion under his or her nose.

5 Repeat the test with pieces of apple and pear. What do you notice about the results?

Cells on our tongues called taste buds detect different flavors. Here is an experiment to find out where your taste buds are.

Where are our taste buds?

1 Place each food item into a paper cup. Using the marker, label each cup according to what it contains.

Difficult – 5
– 4
Moderate – 3
– 2
Easy – 1

You will need:
- A teaspoon of salt
- A teaspoon of sugar
- A teaspoon of lemon juice
- A teaspoon of ground coffee
- Four paper cups
- A marker
- Four popsicle sticks

salt

sugar

lemon juice

Ground Coffee

2 Dip a popsicle stick into the cup with the lemon juice. Place the stick on the tip, back, and sides of your tongue. On which part of the tongue do you taste the sour lemon juice?

3 Repeat the test with the other food items. Use different popsicle sticks for each food item (wet them with water first). Take note of which parts of the tongue taste the salt, the sweetness of the sugar, and the bitterness of the ground coffee.

Smell and taste

In the *What Am I Really Eating?* experiment, you noticed that your friend smelled the food under his or her nose much better than he or she tasted the food being chewed. This is because our sense of smell is stronger than our sense of taste. Our noses are more sensitive and able to pick up smells better than our tongues can taste.

There are four main flavors that the tongue can taste: sweet, sour, salty, and bitter. Different parts of the tongue detect different flavors. The front of the tongue detects sweet and salty flavors, while the sides of the tongue are sensitive to sour flavors. The back of the tongue tastes bitter flavors well.

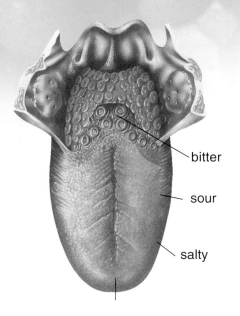

bitter

sour

salty

sweet

How do we smell with our noses and taste with our tongues?

Inside our noses are cells called olfactory cells from which tiny hairs grow. These hairs detect the chemicals that make up odors. The hairs then send the information along the nerves to the brain, which recognizes the smell as one it knows, or as a new smell.

The tasting ability of the tongue comes from tiny bumps on the tongue called taste buds. There are different kinds of taste buds for each of the four flavors. When we chew, saliva, a watery solution that is made by our mouths, dissolves the chemicals in the food. The taste buds detect these chemicals and send information to the brain. Together with the smell, the flavor of the food is detected.

QUIZTIME

How many taste buds are there on an adult's tongue?

Answer: An adult's tongue has up to 10,000 taste buds! Babies' tongues usually have more taste buds than adults' tongues. As we grow older, the number of taste buds decreases.

Did you know?

There are about 40 million hairs in our noses that enable us to detect smells. A dog has even more! A dog has about two billion hairs in its nose! These hairs give a dog a very good sense of smell and allow them to detect smells we cannot. Some dogs (*page 10*) are specially trained by police to smell drugs and bombs.

LOSING YOUR SENSE OF SMELL

We can lose our sense of smell as we grow older. Brain injury can also damage our sense of smell because the brain can no longer process the information from the olfactory cells. Losing our sense of smell can be dangerous because we may not be able to detect harmful gas leaks or smoke from fires.

Touch and feel

The skin on our hands and body has little **receptors** that can feel if something is rough, smooth, cold, or hot. The skin on our fingertips is especially sensitive. Blind people use their fingertips to read words written in **Braille**. See how well you can read with your fingertips!

Braille alphabet

Difficult — 5
— 4
Moderate — 3
— 2
Easy — 1

You will need:
- A ballpoint pen
- A piece of construction paper
- A friend
- A scarf

1 Use the pen to write a three-letter word on the piece of paper. Each letter has to be about ¹/₂ inch (1 cm) from the next letter.

2 Using the point of the pen, press dots along the outline of each letter on the back of the paper.

3 Blindfold your friend with the scarf and see if he or she can identify the word by feeling the raised dots.

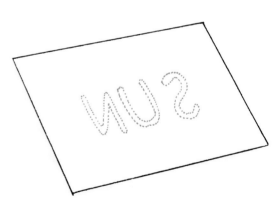

Our sense of touch gets less and less sensitive over time. Try this experiment!

Cold, hot, or warm?

Difficult — 5
— 4
Moderate — 3
— 2
Easy — 1

You will need:
- A bowl of warm water
- A bowl of tap water
- A bowl of ice-cold water
- A table

1 Place the three bowls of water in a row on the table with the tap water in the middle.

2 Put one hand in the warm water, and the other hand in the cold water. Leave your hands in the water for about one minute.

3 Quickly put both hands in the tap water. What do you feel? Leave them there for another minute. How do your hands feel now?

How good is your sense of touch?

Did your friend guess the word correctly in the *Braille Alphabet* experiment? Our fingertips are very good at feeling the details of an object. By moving our fingertips all over the surface of an object, our brain pieces together the information it collects to create a picture of what the object might be.

The Braille alphabet was invented by a fifteen-year-old blind man named Louis Braille. Thanks to him, blind children can read books such as *Cinderella* (*above*) in Braille.

Our sense of touch becomes less sensitive over time. At the start of the *Cold, Hot, or Warm?* experiment, the hand in the cold water felt cold and the hand in the warm water felt warm. After a minute, both hands got used to the sensation, and they did not feel the **temperature** anymore. When both hands were placed in the tap water, the hand that had been in the cold water felt the water as hot, while the other hand that was in the warm water felt it as cold water! After a minute, both hands felt that the water was at room temperature, because the hands got used to the temperature of the water.

How do we feel things?

The receptors on our skin detect different sensations on the skin such as heat, pressure, and pain. There are different kinds of receptors for each of these sensations. When activated, the receptors send nerve signals to the brain, and the brain tries to recognize the object the fingers are touching.

From the senses to the brain

René Descartes (1596–1650; *below*), a French philosopher, was one of the earliest people to ask

how our brains interpret the information our senses receive about the world around us. He found that signals from sensory nerves in the nervous system traveled to the spinal cord and caused body movements. Descartes thought that the pineal gland, an organ in the brain, was the main place where sensory information was interpreted and translated into body movements. Signals were then sent from the pineal gland to other parts of the body.

QUIZTIME

Where do you think the least sensitive part of your body is?

lips
tongue
back
knees

Answer: The skin on your back is the least sensitive. The lips and the tongue are the most sensitive.

Did you know?

In each fingertip, there are about one hundred touch receptors. This is why our fingertips are so sensitive. Our tongues are also very sensitive, but have more receptors for pain than for other sensations. Now you know why it is so painful when you bite your tongue.

When athletes (*left*) feel pain in their bodies, it may be a sign that they are not doing their exercises in the correct way.

PAIN CAN SAVE YOU

Pain receptors are **nerve endings** spread out over the skin of our bodies. Our bodies have a higher number of pain receptors than receptors for other sensations. Our sharp sense of pain helps warn us of danger. We can feel pain, so we know that the heat of fire can burn us and sharp objects can cut us. Without our sense of pain, we could get injured very badly in our everyday activities, because we will not be aware that we are getting hurt!

What happens to food after we eat it?

Difficult — 5
— 4
Moderate — 3
— 2
Easy — 1

You will need:
• A piece of rope 20 feet (6.5 m) long
• A friend
• A measuring tape or ruler
• A piece of chalk

T he body digests or breaks food down into substances that it needs.

Measuring food's journey

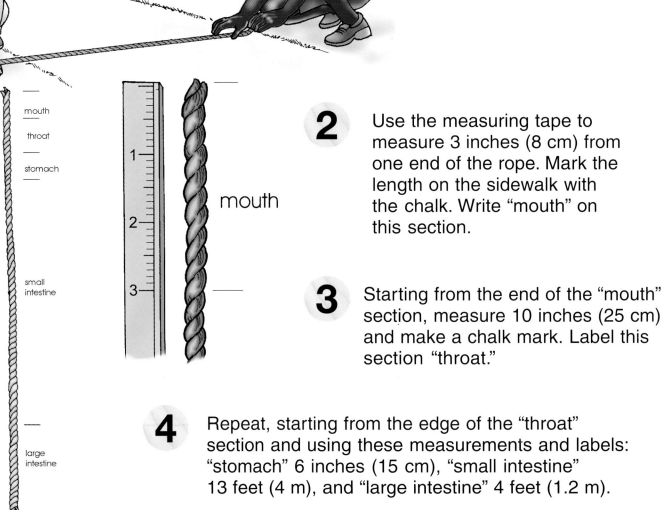

1 Choose a long, flat stretch of sidewalk. Hold one end of the rope and have your friend stretch the rope to its fullest length. Lay the rope down on the sidewalk.

mouth
throat
stomach

small intestine

large intestine

mouth

2 Use the measuring tape to measure 3 inches (8 cm) from one end of the rope. Mark the length on the sidewalk with the chalk. Write "mouth" on this section.

3 Starting from the end of the "mouth" section, measure 10 inches (25 cm) and make a chalk mark. Label this section "throat."

4 Repeat, starting from the edge of the "throat" section and using these measurements and labels: "stomach" 6 inches (15 cm), "small intestine" 13 feet (4 m), and "large intestine" 4 feet (1.2 m).

Congratulations! You have just plotted out the journey that food takes from when it enters your mouth to when your body turns it into waste. What happens to food while it is in your body? Try this experiment to find out!

Breaking down food

1 Squeeze tomato juice onto both pieces of cloth. Leave to dry.

Difficult — 5
    — 4
Moderate — 3
    — 2
Easy — 1

You will need:
- A tomato
- Two pieces of cotton cloth
- Laundry detergent that contains enzymes
- Two large bowls of warm water

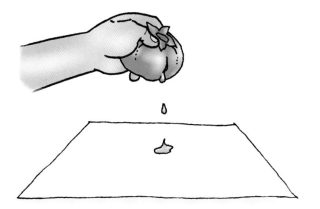

2 Add a scoop of laundry detergent to one of the bowls of warm water.

3 Place one piece of tomato-stained cloth in each bowl. What happens to the tomato stain in the bowl that contains laundry detergent?

Digestive system

Our bodies need the food that we eat to give us energy, help us grow, and to repair and build new cells. In the *Measuring Food's Journey* experiment, you saw that food travels a distance of about 20 feet (6.5 m) inside our bodies. Food enters the mouth, where it is mixed with saliva to break it down so that it can be swallowed. The smaller pieces of food travel down our throats to our stomachs. In the stomach, food pieces are mixed with liquid that the stomach produces to break food into smaller bits. This liquid contains enzymes, which are substances that break food down into a soupy liquid. In the experiment *Breaking Down Food*, you noticed that the enzymes in the laundry detergent helped to dissolve the tomato stain on the cloth. The same thing happens when enzymes and acids in our stomach juices break down food.

From the stomach, the soupy liquid moves to the small intestine. The small intestine is about 13 feet (4 m) long and is coiled up. Inside the small intestine, nutrients are absorbed into our blood and taken to the **liver** to be stored and distributed around the body. The food pieces that our bodies do not need travel from the small intestine to the large intestine, where they are stored until they leave our bodies as waste.

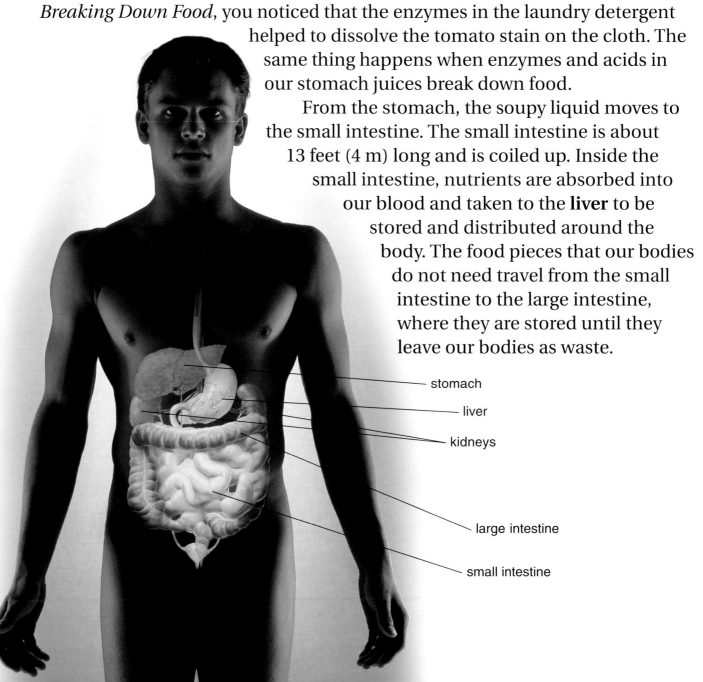

stomach

liver

kidneys

large intestine

small intestine

Can you stomach this?

Captain William Beaumont (1785–1853; *left*) was a U.S. army surgeon. He had a patient who had been shot in the stomach. While the patient was healing, Beaumont had the opportunity to do tests on the juices that the stomach makes, and study the way that food is digested. In one experiment, Beaumont tied tiny pieces of food to a silk string, and placed the food in the wound in the patient's stomach. The pieces of food, including beef, cabbage, and bread, were left in the hole in the patient's stomach for up to five hours, before Beaumont pulled them out.

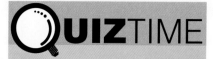

QUIZTIME

How long does it take for food to travel through our digestive systems?

Answer: It takes about 24 hours for food to be digested. Food spends about four hours in the stomach, six hours in the small intestine, and fourteen hours or more in the large intestine.

Did you know?

You have three main types of teeth in your mouth (*right*). Incisors are the flat-topped teeth in the front of your mouth that cut food. Canines are the pointy, sharp teeth that rip and tear food apart. Molars are the wide, flat teeth at the back of your mouth that crush food into small pieces.

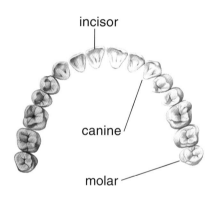

incisor

canine

molar

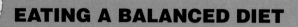

EATING A BALANCED DIET

The kinds of food we eat are important to our health. We need to eat a balanced diet that includes proteins, found in meat, dairy products, and beans; carbohydrates, found in breads and cereals; and vitamins and minerals, found in fruits and vegetables (*left*).

How not to fall...

Our sense of balance helps us walk and run without falling. How do we control our balance? All things, including humans, have a center of **gravity**. The center of gravity is the point where all the weight of the object balances. Where is the center of gravity?

Finding balance

Difficult – 5
– 4
Moderate – 3
– 2
Easy – 1

You will need:
- A ruler with measured markings in inches (or centimeters)
- A notebook
- A pencil or pen
- A friend
- An eraser

1 Place the ruler on two fingers, with one end of the ruler on one finger of each hand.

2 Slowly slide your fingers toward each other, keeping the ruler horizontal. In the notebook, record the number on the ruler where your fingers meet. This is the center of gravity.

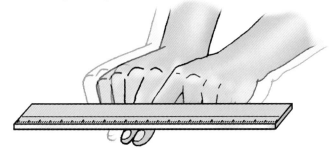

3 Repeat step 1. This time, ask your friend to place the eraser on one side of the ruler.

4 Keeping the ruler horizontal, slide your fingers together again. Record the number where your fingers meet. The center of gravity is not always at the center of the ruler!

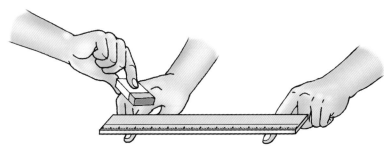

How do you find the center of gravity of an irregularly shaped object?

Find the center of gravity

Difficult — 5
— 4
Moderate — 3
— 2
Easy — 1

You will need:
- Scissors
- A piece of cardboard
- A screwdriver
- A piece of string
- Two pencils
- A small rock

1 Cut the cardboard into any shape, as irregular as you wish. Using the sharp end of the screwdriver, make five holes at the edges of the cardboard. Try to space the holes equally from each other.

2 Push the point of a pencil through one of the holes. Tie one end of the string around the pencil and the other end around the rock.

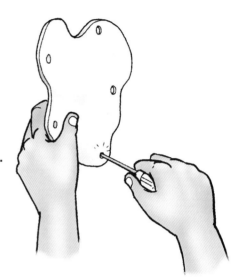

3 Hang the cardboard and the rock by holding the pencil as shown in the diagram. Using the other pencil, draw a line along the string.

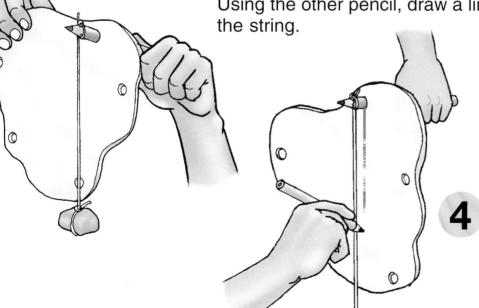

4 Repeat steps 2 and 3 with the other holes.

21

A balancing act

In the experiment *Find the Center of Gravity*, the lines you drew met at a single point. This point was the center of gravity of the cardboard piece. To check this, try balancing the cardboard piece on the point of the pen. The cardboard piece stays flat on the tip of the pen! The center of gravity is where the force of gravity acting down on the cardboard equals the opposite force of the pen holding the cardboard up.

The cerebellum is the part in the brain that controls movement, posture, and balance. The cerebellum receives information from our moving muscles and then sends it to the other parts of the body. If the cerebellum is damaged, walking, writing, and speaking become difficult.

Our ears are also important in helping us keep our balance! A semicircular canal in the inner ear contains a special fluid and hair cells. When we move our bodies, our heads move, moving the fluid in the canal as a result. The moving fluid in turn moves the hair cells which send messages to the brain. These messages tell the brain if the body is out of balance.

Body machine

Italian mathematician Giovanni Alfonso Borelli (1608–1679; *below*) was one of the first scientists to study human and animal anatomy by examining simple machines. He argued that human and animal bones worked like levers and pulleys and the muscles behaved like elastic bands tying the bones together. Scientists used Borelli's ideas to help them understand the pumping of the human heart, and how birds fly and fish swim.

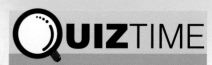

QUIZTIME

What does the brain look like and how much does it weigh?

Answer: The brain is about the size of a large grapefruit, pinkish-gray in color, and with many folds, or wrinkles. It is also very soft. An adult brain weighs an average of three pounds (1.4 kg).

Did you know?

Your muscles help you to balance. Some muscles work in pairs. When one muscle moves, another adjusts itself to keep you balanced. Your brain (*right*) learned how to control these muscles when you were very young.

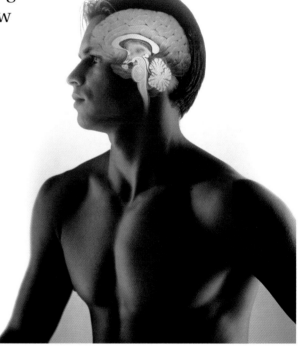

When we move very fast, many images pass before our eyes. Sometimes, our brains cannot process the information from our eyes fast enough. When that happens, we may feel dizzy.

STILL SPINNING?

Why do we feel dizzy after we stop spinning? When we spin, the fluid in our ears starts to spin too. When we stop, the fluid continues to spin, which tricks the brain into thinking that the body is still moving. This is why we feel dizzy and lose our balance!

How warm is it inside our bodies?

The body produces heat when it burns food for energy. The body temperature of a healthy person is around 98.6°F (37°C). Is our body temperature always the same?

Does my temperature change?

1 Measure your temperature every five hours throughout the day.

You will need:
- An oral thermometer
- A pencil or pen
- A notebook

2 Record your temperature readings in the notebook.

3 Compare the readings at the end of the day. What do you see?

TIME OF DAY | TEMPERATURE

When we exercise, we feel hot and we perspire. Does this mean our body temperature has increased?

Hot and sweaty

Difficult — 5
— 4
Moderate — 3
— 2
Easy — 1

You will need:
• An oral thermometer
• A pencil or pen
• A notebook

1 Measure your body temperature just before you play a ball game or run. Record it in the notebook.

2 Immediately after you exercise, measure your temperature again. Do you observe any differences in temperature?

Controlling the heat

In the *Does My Temperature Change?* experiment, you noticed that the temperature of the human body changes only slightly throughout the day. This is true even after you exercise. In the experiment *Hot and Sweaty*, your body temperature should not have changed more than 0.1°F (0.06°C). Our bodies are very good at controlling our temperature, even though the temperature outside our bodies might change greatly.

When it is cold outside, we shiver and goose bumps rise on our skin. Goose bumps are puckers in our skin caused by tiny muscles under the skin working to make the hair stand on end. The standing hair traps air next to our skin. Air is a poor **conductor** of heat, so the heat produced by our bodies remains next to our skin and keeps us warm.

When it is hot outside, we sweat, or perspire. Sweat is a salty liquid produced by cells under our skin. As sweat **evaporates**, it draws heat away from the body. The same thing happens when we exercise. During a workout, we work our muscles more than usual, and this produces heat. Sweating helps us to cool down.

What happens if it is too hot or too cold?

Goose bumps (*below*) can help warm our bodies if the temperature changes slightly. Extreme temperatures can be dangerous to the body, because the body can only control its temperature within a certain temperature range. If body temperature drops below 96°F (35.6°C), the heart will fail, resulting in death. This condition is called hypothermia. When our body temperature is too high, we may suffer from heat stroke, a severe illness which causes vomiting and fainting.

What should you do if someone is suffering from heat stroke?

Answer: Quickly take the person to a cool place, and sponge him or her with cold water. Call a doctor immediately. People suffering from heat stroke may die if they do not receive prompt medical attention.

Did you know?
Reptiles, which are cold-blooded animals such as snakes, lizards, turtles, and tortoises (*left*), cannot produce body heat. Reptiles heat themselves by absorbing sunlight, which is why you often see reptiles basking in the sun. On cold days, reptiles do not move much because they are trying not to waste their body heat.

COOLING WATER

Having enough water in your body is very important on a hot day, especially when you are playing sports. If you are dehydrated, or lack water in your body, the risk of heat stroke is higher as your body may not produce enough sweat to cool you down. So make sure you drink plenty of water on a hot day, as well as during exercise.

Our hearts and lungs

The heart is an involuntary muscle, which means that it works without us realizing it. Together, our heart and lungs supply oxygen-rich blood to the body.

Balloon lung

■ **Ask an adult for help**

Difficult — 5
— 4
Moderate — 3
— 2
Easy — 1

You will need:
- A clear plastic soda bottle
- A pocketknife
- Two balloons
- An elastic band
- Scissors
- Tape

1 Ask an adult to slice the bottle in half across the middle using the pocketknife.

2 Cover the neck of the bottle with one of the balloons as shown in the diagram. Secure the balloon with the elastic band.

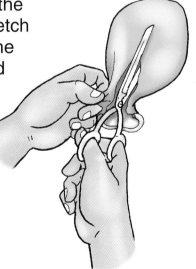

3 Using the scissors, cut the other balloon open. Stretch the rubber material of the balloon over the cut end of the bottle, and tape it in place.

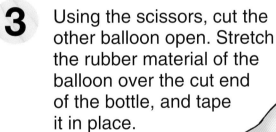

4 Push the rubber piece at the bottom into the bottle. Watch what happens to the balloon at the top of the bottle.

Is our heartbeat the same all the time?

Listen to the beat!

Difficult — 5
— 4
Moderate — 3
— 2
Easy — 1

You will need:
- The cardboard tube from an empty paper towel roll
- A friend
- A stopwatch
- A pencil or pen
- A notebook

1 Place one end of the cardboard tube on the left side of your friend's chest, where the heart is. Put your ear next to the other end of the tube and listen. Do you hear your friend's heart beating?

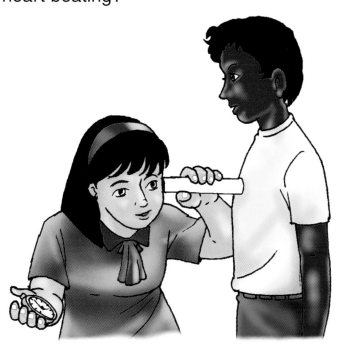

2 Start the stopwatch. Count the number of beats you hear. Stop counting when the stopwatch tells you one minute is over. Record the number of beats in the notebook.

NUMBER OF BEATS PER MINUTE

How do our lungs and hearts work?

We do not just breathe with our lungs, we breathe with the help of our diaphragms as well. The diaphragm is a dome-shaped muscle just below the lungs. Both the diaphragm and lungs are found in the chest cavity.

The bottle represented the lungs in the experiment *Balloon Lung*, and the rubber piece stood for the diaphragm. When we exhale, or blow air out from our lungs, the diaphragm curves upward, increasing the **air pressure** inside the chest cavity. This pushes on the lungs and forces air out. You saw this process in the model lung when the balloon inflated as you pushed in the rubber piece. When we breathe in, the diaphragm flattens. This creates space in the chest cavity, allowing air from outside our body to move into the lungs. In the experiment, the balloon deflated when you stopped pushing the rubber piece.

Our heart is a muscle that pumps blood to all parts of the body. The heartbeat you heard in the experiment *Listen to the Beat* was the sound of your friend's heart pumping. Our heartbeat depends on how active we are. After exercise, the heart beats faster, as it tries to get more blood to our working muscles. When we are sleeping, our hearts beat slower because all our muscles are resting.

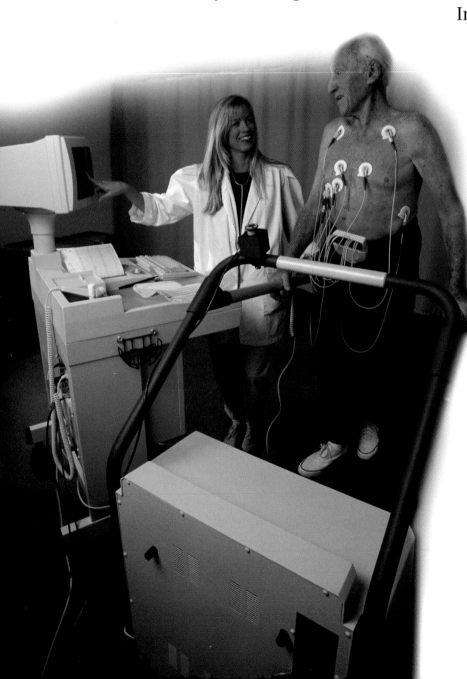

Did you know that each time your heart beats it releases some electricity? Doctors measure this electricity using an electrocardiogram (ECG) machine (*left*). ECG machines help doctors monitor if their patients' hearts are beating regularly.

The heart and lung connection

There are millions of tiny **blood vessels** called capillaries in our lungs. When we breathe, the capillaries pick up oxygen. The body uses the oxygen from the blood and releases a waste product, a gas called carbon dioxide. Vessels carry blood that is rich in carbon dioxide to the heart. The heart pumps the blood to the lungs, which release the carbon dioxide as we exhale. The blood takes in more oxygen and flows from the lungs back to the heart.

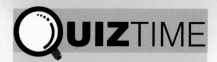

QUIZTIME

How big is your heart?

Answer: The heart is about the size of your fist. As your body develops, the heart grows in size with your fist.

Did you know?

Your heart may be only the size of your fist, but it pumps about 2,000 gallons (7,571 liters) of blood each day! In a person's lifetime, his or her heart will beat 2.5 billion times and pump about 50 million gallons (189.3 million liters) of blood!

The heart has a left side and a right side (*left*). The left side of the heart pumps blood containing carbon dioxide to the lungs, while the right side of the heart pumps oxygen-rich blood to the rest of the body. Blood flowing through the body is known as circulation.

X-rays (*below*) are a common method doctors use to help them study the heart and lungs of their patients. X-rays are rays of light that can penetrate solids.

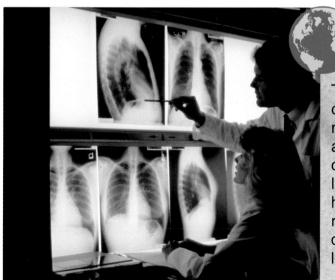

KILLER SMOKE

There are 4,000 **chemical compounds** in cigarette smoke, and 43 of these compounds may cause cancer! One of these is tar, which is a black, sticky substance. When we breathe in cigarette smoke, it destroys the cilia hairs that line our **airways**. These cilia hairs prevent harmful chemicals in the air we breathe from reaching our lungs. When the cilia hairs are destroyed, substances such as tar enter our lungs and kill the cells in our lungs.

Glossary

air pressure (page 30): The weight of air pressing down on an object.

airways (page 31): The passages through which air travels from the nose and mouth to the lungs.

blood vessels (page 31): Tubes that carry blood through the body.

Braille (page 12): A system of writing made up of a combination of raised dots which represent letters, punctuation marks, and numbers.

cells (page 7): Small units that are the building blocks of all living things. Humans have billions of cells that make up our bodies.

chemical compound (page 31): Two or more substances that are combined to make a different substance.

conductor (page 26): A material that carries energy from one place to another.

evaporate (page 26): Change from a liquid state into a gas.

gravity (page 20): The force of attraction that works on objects to pull them to Earth.

liver (page 18): A large gland that purifies chemicals in the body, and processes, stores, and distributes digested food.

molecules (page 4): The smallest unit of a substance.

muscles (page 7): Body parts that are designed to contract. Muscles are made up of muscle tissue. Tissues are a collection of similar cells that perform one main function.

nerve cells (page 7): Long, thin cells that carry messages from one cell to another.

nerve endings (page 15): The branch-like ends of nerves. In pain receptors the nerve endings are not covered by a protective layer of tissue.

nerve signals (page 6): Chemical signals that carry information the senses receive about our environment to the brain.

receptors (page 12): Cells that are sensitive to stimuli, or anything that produces a response in the body. Nerves connect receptors to the spinal cord.

temperature (page 14): The hotness or coldness of something.

Index